For the Life of Me

Franklin S White

Poetry for Over the Hill Hippies

DORRANCE PUBLISHING CO
EST. 1920
PITTSBURGH, PENNSYLVANIA 15238

The contents of this work, including, but not limited to, the accuracy of events, people, and places depicted; opinions expressed; permission to use previously published materials included; and any advice given or actions advocated are solely the responsibility of the author, who assumes all liability for said work and indemnifies the publisher against any claims stemming from publication of the work.

All Rights Reserved
Copyright © 2023 by Franklin S White

No part of this book may be reproduced or transmitted, downloaded, distributed, reverse engineered, or stored in or introduced into any information storage and retrieval system, in any form or by any means, including photocopying and recording, whether electronic or mechanical, now known or hereinafter invented without permission in writing from the publisher.

Dorrance Publishing Co
585 Alpha Drive
Pittsburgh, PA 15238
Visit our website at *www.dorrancebookstore.com*

ISBN: 979-8-8868-3218-1
eISBN: 979-8-8868-3791-9

Franklin S White
(1949-1967)

Franklin S. White had what would be called a very short life span; life for him ended at the age of 18. Yet while he lived, he expressed himself in a way that will long be remembered. It is such a pity to have someone with his great talent to end life at such an early age.

If death would not have called to him that one last time, and he were alive today, he would have become one of the great poets of our time. His style was that of Bob Dylan, The Beatles, and Ferlinghette, yet, it was a style all his own. He was the type of person that wrote what he felt and felt what he wrote.

The contents of the book you are about to read holds the major poems that White wrote before his death. Although you may not understand or agree with what he has to say in some of his works, you will find yourself captivated by his style and his manner of writing.

But first read the book, and if you have to, re-read it and then decide, would he and could he have been a great poet? I knew F S White probably better than anyone else in the entire world, and I think that after reading this book you will be able to answer the above question with a very positive "yes."

DEDICATION

This book is dedicated to all Viet Nam veterans, those living and those who have left this earth.

PRELUDE

Past is there,
Present is boring,
Future is exciting.
But, eventually, the exciting future,
Becomes the boring present; which
Becomes the past, which is there.

TABLE OF CONTENTS

Happening in One Day 1
Two Hearts (one Heart in Love) 2
Spanish Lace 3
Substantial Circumstances 5
I Loved You Once 6
Contemplation 7
We'll Meet 8
When my Grave I Lay 9
Who Will Go With Me? 10
Beauty 11
Would it Make Any Difference? 12
Difference In People 13
Withstand 14
Snow And Wind 15
Ahaggarr (Straw Isle) 16
If 18
A Poem From The Heart 19
The Death of Love 20
Death of One Man 21
The End of the Earth 22
Today and Tomorrow 23
Girls of Sin 24
I Light A Candle 25
Sonnet To A Chair 26
Into Each Life 27
Life Goes On 29
Wheels 30
Life, Death, and Love 32
Why Not? 34

Come Into My House, Death 37
Sunglass Hobbits 38
Watch Out: You're Crazy 40
Argument: Two Sides 42
Blind and Deaf 43
Color Me Red 44
The Mockingbird 45
Pre And Post 47
Catch Me 48
Come! 49
Silent 52
Like A... 53
Time 54
To Exist Forever Is To Die But Once 55
Here I 56
Dance, Angeles, Dance 57
Blood 58
A Mess of Words 59
The Room 60
Untitled Symphony 61
As The Night is Silent 62
My Wonderings 62
But Never Of The Future 64

Happening in One Day

The wind is howling today.
The steps, coming up from the field, are wet,
And we travel down the road opposite the river.
The chairs in our room are arranged in opposite order;
Our feet touch the floor only at the bottoms of our shoes.
A blue bird dies.

A deaf mute is understanding all he hears.
He speaks,
"Don't talk to me, because I can't see you,
And quit baying at my heels like a hungry dog."
Then he dies away with the early morning dew,
Never to return until tomorrow.

A dead dog is sleeping by the edge of the road;
He awakes, and sheepishly slimes away into nothing;
Carrying with him all the sins of his day.
While he is dying once more he howls at the wind;
The wind howls back,
And another day begins.

Franklin S White

Two Hearts (One Heart in Love)

Two hearts, one heart in love
Two hearts, she doesn't think of-
Me as the guy she always could love
If she tried.

She loved me once, and then I said good-bye
She loved me twice, I started to cry.

Two hearts, one heart in love
Two hearts, she doesn't think of
Me as the guy she always could love
If she would,
Because she could.

Two hearts, one heart in love
She's the one I always think of.
And she's the one I really do love,
Because I do.

Two hearts, one heart in love
Two hearts, she doesn't think of-
Herself as the girl I really do love
And me as the guy she said that she loved.

Two hearts, one heart in love
Two hearts, one love begins to fade.
One love changes for another
And one love stays in love with the other.

Two hearts, one heart in love
Two hearts, she doesn't think of-
Me as the guy she always could love
If she would,
Because she could.

For the Life of Me

Spanish Lace

Spanish lace of blue and gold,
Cannot grab you, cannot hold;
You're too far beyond the realms of mind
Your senseless knowledge, your thoughts can't bind-
Can't bind together and form a noose,
To tie your hands and not let you loose.
You're a free man of spirit
So listen while you hear it
As we tell you of life gone by
Because at least once every man mist die.

Spanish lace that cannot be bought,
Like everything else is always sought;
Like human freedom, it's always looked for
And you won't and it in a neighborhood drug store.
A drug store is a place where you can by drugs
And not Spanish lace made into rugs.
In a drug store you find all types of pills,
It's not a place to buy freedom for the price of dollar bills;
Freedom comes from peace at hand
And you cannot retain it in a topless can.

Spanish lace is bought by the yard;
In a deck, ace is the highest card.
Freedom is the highest form of life
And you can end it all with a sharp knife
To kill yourself is not to be free,
You'll just walk around and cease to be.
Retain your freedom as long as you can,
And take long walks throughout the land;
And capture natures' beauty as it really looks
Because you won't find it in any written books.

Franklin S White

Capture nature as it really is
As time belongs to her, it never was his;
Nature is all that is beautiful
As wine in a silver glass, a cupful:
Nature started the world, and it too
Will end it, end me and end you.

Spanish lace of blue and gold
Is always new, it is never old.
Cover your life with only Spanish lace,
And it could turn out to be a waste,

Because freedoms screen like door
Will haunt your life forever moor—
Haunt your life to be free
Because it is all that you want to be.

For the Life of Me

Substantial Circumstances

Under no possible circumstances shall my mind be rearranged,
Nothing will be blotted out, rewritten, scraped, or even changed;
It shall be as it ever was, for my memory will stay
With me and by me, accompanying me through every new and passing day.
It shall remain as my constant companion through life and death,
To keep me going and doing things until my last dying breath.

I shall always think about matters of oppressing manner,
To guide me strong, as I go on my way and carry my worthless banner.
And under all circumstances shall my illustrious mind unwind:
My clear thoughts of insanity will pass before me at all times.
And I shall never give a substantial downgrading to any man,
If he be far from his native home or relatively close at hand.

Franklin S White

I Loved You Once

I loved you once, for the rest of my life,
And I did you wrong by wanting you for my wife;
Please forgive me for that one great sin,
Because it brought forth the relationship that we are now in.

I love you now and I always will,
And I'm sorry that the loves we had I did kill.
Please give my love just one more try,
And I know that with your help, our love will survive;
Just let me love you and you like me,
And see how good for each other it would be.

Contemplation

Come out from behind your pretensions;
Don't hide behind that window,
Because even you can exist through immorality.
Social interaction is a learned process.
You are sinking beneath the realms of humanity.

No, you can't marry my daughter!
Do you enjoy sitting on a garbage can?
Count the number of times you've been born,
Then add three to get your age.

The goose is infested with life.

No, you can't play with my Viet Nam war game!
Our favorite tree is dead in the summer snow.
Quit banging on that pop bottle,
Count to nine.
?Como esta usted?

We'll Meet

We'll meet again
When all is gone,
It will be no sin
For the race we'll have won.

We'll meet once more
Far across the sea,
And on a distant shore
You'll look for me.

We'll meet someday.
And when we do,
I can, if I may
Say "Hi" to you.

We'll meet sometime
And if we don't,
I'll buy the wine
And cry then I won't.

We'll meet as friends
Or maybe as foes,
And then again
Maybe as beaus.

We'll meet somewhere
And the we will go,
To a place of beauty fair
That we won't know.

We'll meet I think
And maybe then too,
We won't.
So take up your cup and drink,
And it's been nice knowing you.

For the Life of Me

When My Grave I Lay
When my grave I lay,
As dead as I can afford
And shut up in a casket of iron
So as to preserve my body,
Will I lay alone?

When my grave I lay,
Sleeping an endless sleep
And dreaming unspoken dreams
Unspoken because no one is around to hear them,
Will my friends come see me?

When my grave I lay,
With death all around me
And no second life before me
Except to grow old with time, or remain young,
Will my allies rejoice me?

When my grave I lay,
Cushioned by natures' sweet embrace
And surrounded by white satin and lace,
And covered in garments of the times,
Will I be remembered?

Franklin S White

Who Will Go With Me?

Who will go with me,
When I go to steal the Persian King?
No one will go.
And who will want to shake in the spending of ransom?
Everyone will want to.
Because no one wants to get his hands dirty,
But is willing to enjoy the pleasures of someone else's.

Who will go with me,
And risk his life for freedom?
Not one person will volunteer.
But when I ask who wants freedom for his country
Everyone raises his hand and says, "Me."
This is because everyone wants freedom,
But they want someone to get it for them,
So they don't have to work for it.

And who will go with me to scout out new frontiers?
Everyone is too busy to go.
But who wants to live in new and better areas?
Everyone does, of course.
These people are "pleasure seekers"
And they want everyone except themselves to work for something;
And when it is achieved,
They want to share in the "spoils of victory"
And they go away mad when refused.

For the Life of Me

Beauty

It is said that beauty is only skin deep.
But I wonder which would be better;
Beauty on top where it shows,
Or beauty inside where it glows?

But why should I worry,
For you have both.

Would It Make Any Difference?

Would it make any difference,
If I said I still loved you?
Would you still go and leave me alone?
And if I said I'll always think of you,
Would you still go and leave your home?

Would it make any difference,
If you took my heart
And treated it like a toy?
And if you pull us apart,
Would you ever come back to this boy?

Would it make any difference?
Because if it won't
Then I won't try again
To capture your heart as my own.

Difference In People

Some went and some came back,
Some never left;
Some were rich and some were poor,
Some were independence bereft;
Some were single and some did separate,
Some were wed;
Some were alone and some were happy,
Some were dead.

At one time all were together,
Then some went their separate and own different ways;
All found fame in one way or another,
And found that fortune pays.

Some went East and some went West,
Few traveled North and South;
Some were different and some were not,
But few found the river's mouth.

Withstand

Withstand pressure of the ages
    and you will live eternally
    save time and spend it when
    you've nothing else to do.
Withstand the dark ages
    and you will see light become dim
    understand all you see and hear
    and you become hated by all.
Withstand all ignorance
    on the part of fellow man
    ask questions of no interest
    and people will marvel at your
    disobedience to government.
Withstand the zodiac
    and play among the stars
    be ignorant to everything
    so people will want to be friends.
Withstand everything
    and you will die unwanted.

For the Life of Me

Snow and Wind

It is near the fall of the year
And snow is on the wry.
And when it comes, the snow will say,
"Hey, I am snow and I have come-
Come to cover the earth with a soft white blanket."

Along with snow comes
The wind.
And when it comes, the wind will say,
"Hey, I am wind and I have come-
Come to make it cold."

And when these two forces come together,
Be they good or bad,
You can be assured of one thing,
That is;
It's going to be cold and wet and white
And really one hell of a mess,

Franklin S White

Ahaggar (Straw Isle)

Come with me,
And together we will go;
Through woods, over rivers, and around valleys,
Until we come to my favorite sitting place.
Here we will sit forever,
And we will know no time;
For in this place you exist in any form you want.
What is this place I speak of?
It is my favorite dwelling place,
It is Straw Isle.

I come here when troubled,
And bring all my problems, by the truckload
Here you are only what you want
And no one bothers you;
Because no one else is here-
Because no one else knows of this place but me.
Where is this place I speak of?
It is my favorite thinking place,
It is Straw Isle.

Come, together we shall find ourselves
And no other place will exist to us
We will be alone with each other,
And alone with ourselves.
Here I find complete happiness
And you shall find it too;
When you leave, you leave all troubles and worries behind you.
Where is this place I speak of?
It is my favorite existing place.
It is Straw Isle,

For the Life of Me

You can stay as long as you desire
For time exists here not;
And when you leave you will be in complete happiness.
I go there as often as I want to
And stay until I am ready to leave
I never tell where this place is,
But you may come, only if you want.
Where is this place I speak of?
It is my favorite staying place,
It is Straw Isle,

As I walk through fields of soft grass
I feel a certain stillness in the air
It is a silent stillness,
Without violence or hate.
Also there is no love, as in emotion
The only love is in that of nature.
The silence is only broken by whistling winds and singing birds.
Where is this piece I speak of?
It is my favorite quite place,
It is Straw Isle.

We will lie among yellow flowers
And watch small trees grow;
They will stand tall and green forever,
Because there is no seasonal change there,
The only change is in attitude.
You come with feelings of trouble and leave with feelings of contentment,
You are content with yourself, if nothing else.
But where is this place I speak of?
It is my favorite place of refuge, and it can be yours too,
It is Straw Isle.

If

If, when I see you I shy away,
                it's not because
                              I hate you; I love you.
If, when I catch your eye,
                I don't speak,
                              It's only because I don't want to cry.
If, I ignore your total existence,
                it's not because
                              I dislike you; I adore you.
Don't say "Hi" because I won't speak;
                all I could say is
                          "I LOVE YOU."

For the Life of Me

A POEM From the Heart

When I met her I felt so glad,
If she leaves me I'll feel so bad;
I've always loved her from the start,
But now I know it's from the heart.

When we met both were already taken
So our feelings for each other were all forsaken;
As time went by and our likes for others swayed,
Our feelings for each other had stayed and stayed.

And now we're together, how long no one really knows
But as time goes by our hearts and souls will show;
And if it lasts but a week or two,
My love for her was all but untrue.

Franklin S White

The Death of Love

It was on the sixth of a past November
That we met, oh how well I do remember,
I held her both close and dear to my heart;
And we vowed to each other that we'd never part.
We built our love on truth of life,
I, as her husband and she as my wife.

As the past went by and the present came nearer,
In our hearts each became dearer
The foundation of our togetherness was built on love;
And we were one in the eyes of the creator above.
Our marriage was faithful because of the love in each heart,
But we never knew in s short time we'd have to part.

Our reality of love didn't last e very long time,
But it was no fault of hers or no fault of mine,
While loving each other we accomplished one important thing;
And that was the joy and contentment a true love can bring.
In loving each other we did no wrong,
And we're still in love even though she is gone.

We lived and loved for less than one year
And now she is gone and I stand alone here,
Here by her grave looking through my tears
At a broken-up existence that should have lasted years.

"The Lord giveth and the Lord taketh away"
And I'll stay with my grievances until that day,
When again we'll be together, and for all time
I can claim again what is rightfully mine.

Death of One Man

Such a violent death I have dies;
Yet on I live,
With haunting memory to those around.
In casket 'neath the ground I lay,
On top it's marked with stone
Yet, no one knows of my passing.
On bed of silk my bones to rest
They walk no more on solid ground;
And on through forever I sleep.

As for my ears, they hear no sound,
And tell my lips of nothing new.
Yet, above me life goes one
My feet ore pierced where once they bled,
My bloody hands are wrapped around me,
And my side has ceased to bleed;
And I am sure of only one thing,
That is, for my enemies I asked forgiveness.

Franklin S White

The End of The Earth

So be it,
Man is now dead and his memory no longer exists
Because there is no one to remember it.
The button was pushed
And the earth was destroyed,
In a few seconds man destroyed
What it had taken him millions of years to build.

But why was it destroyed?
Because one man disagreed with another
And one country disagreed with another
And because the world stood divided,
The free world vs the captured world.

A button was pushed launching a bomb,
Then another and another
Soon the entire world was up in flames.
Some people cried and some people laughed
But eventually they all died;
There was no one left to bury the bodies
So they started to decay.
Then suddenly that was left of the world started to shake
It shook like never before
Then there was such an explosion that every planet in the universe was shaken from its routed path.
The explosion was such like was never heard before and will never be heard again,
For the earth exploded
And its dust scattered to drift endlessly in space.

The inhabitants of other planets were happy-
Happy to see such a violent and corrupt world destroyed by its own people.
Now the rest of the Solar System and Galaxy could live in pence.
So be it,
The end of the earth.

For the Life of Me

Today and Tomorrow

A cup of coffee and a T-bone steak
And you find that the waitress made a mistake.
If your life goes by this way,
Then you live your life day by day.

Girls Of Sin

Mary Jane
loves sugar cane
first thing every morning.
But she does despise
the glow in my eyes
when I touch her soft white body.

Linde Sue
says, "I love you"
at exactly twelve o'clock.
But she hates to her
me say, "I want you, dear"
when first I rise each morning.

I touch their skin
with a fire like touch. I kiss their
lips and walk away
when again we meet
I do the same.
And they enjoy it more.

They love to feel my hands on them,
and then they want to play,
but I don't like their games
so I walk away.

For the Life of Me

I Light A Candle

I light a candle
For each day the moon does shine
And I write a poem
So that I won't forget
The moon and her children
Who rule the night.

I light a candle
For every time the clock strikes twelve
And I sing a song
To help me remember
The clocks' twelve helpers
Who help run the day.

I light a candle
For every song which is sung
And I cheer a cheer
To let me not forget
The notes of the scale
Which make up the music.

I light a candle
Every time I start to forget
The things I should remember.

Franklin S White

Sonnet To A Chair

The chair is a fantastic creature,
That occupies space anywhere;
Fit for pirate, hobo, or preacher.
Any one may sit there.

It stands in one place all day long,
Never complaining a bit.
Over 4,000,000 people can't be wrong,
Because they all want to sit.

It faces the window or faces the wall,
It really doesn't care.
It's at home in a store or at a ball,
No matter where you're at, it's always there.

So to yourself be fair,
And go buy a chair.

Into Each Life

Into each life
Some joy must come,
It may come with moon
Or with sun.
But if you wait and search
You will find it.

Into each life
Troubles will trod.
They come with devils
Or even with GOD.
They may be good and bad
And it's your responsibility to find out which
And then deal accordingly.

Into each life
Responsibilities will fall.
Some days many
Some days none at all.
And you must meet and deal with them
Or they can and will destroy you.

Into each life
Opportunity will come.
It comes only once
Then fades with new sun.
When it comes you must grab it and follow
Or your life is worthless.

Franklin S White

Into each life
A desire will become present.
It comes to kings
Or a lonely peasant.
But it will occur
And you must satisfy it
Or live with it indefinitely.

Into each life
Permanent depth will come,
But only once.
And you must obey its call.

For the Life of Me

Life Goes On

As quick as snow falls,
It melts;
As soon as rain drops,
It dries;
As fast as light travels,
Once it has passed
It is once more dark;
After a person is born,
He must die.

After a sound is heard,
It is forgotten;
When a sight is seen,
It disappears;
As soon as a knife cuts,
Blood runs freely.

But after
Snow melts and rain dries,
After
light passes and someone dies,
After
 Sound is forgotten and sight disappears,
And after blood runs freely,
Somewhere, life still goes on.

Wheels

I.
The turning wheels
Turn upon ray heels
And shape out time
Which is only mine
And destroys day
In a very strange way.

The velvet wheels
Step within my heels
And walk through night
By candle light
And causes slumber
In a chosen number.

The sanguine wheels
Walk beside my heels
And tap out songs
Of rights and wrongs
And turns on heat
To whomever they meet.

The fading wheels
Stroll behind my heels
And they cause me pain
Over and over again
And withstand cold
While they never grow old.

For the Life of Me

II.
The suspicious wheels
Bark and yap at my heels
They speak of hate and sin
And worthless people
They talk of nature
And live off man-made objects.

The intelligent wheels
Hold conversation with my heels
And act like real people
By telling secrets about everything
And put down lies
While using the word "friend."

The wheels of fortune
Are lucky and happy
But not content
They act happy,
but are miserable
Because, like most humans,
They lack contentment.

Franklin S White

Life, Death, and Love

Life is but a stepping stone to death,
And he who dwells on its premises is doomed.
To live alone is to east in eternity with oneself;
Life progresses slowly into nothingness and discreetly into fulfillment.
The world is an ungodly fortune cookie
Whose contents are of plastic and paper-meche'.

To be born is a mistake and to die is the righting of that mistake;
Life and death welk hand in hand;
To live once is to die a thousand times.

Love is a one note symphony;
It cuts with razor sharpness and makes one bleed.

Instant death comes unnoticed and leaves being looked upon by all;
A failure in life is a success in death
Being purposely passed into the gates of Hell.
"Nirvana" is an unknown place to the wicked
And Hell knows no boundaries;
The achievement of grace is the price you must pay for death.

Death will pass before your eyes unnoticed and unwanted
But never the less it is there.
Love is but an unanswered question dreamed about by peasants,
And people who question life shall die, unanswered;
Existence is but a slow form of death
And death is to exist forever.
A man once said, "To die is to live and to live is to die, it is the choice between the lesser of two evils."
To live is ungodly, but to die is divine;
The months passing through a year are numbered.
And the years passing through a man are also numbered.
Please be seated while Berth takes your hand and passes you by yourself.

For the Life of Me

Inorganic matter drifts endlessly in space,
While being prayed upon by death.

Love not, bleed not; for if you love you shall surely bleed.
To love and not be loved is worse than to die and be unnoticed;
A one note symphony is love.
Love only exists to those who cannot afford its misery.

Love has a bite worse than death
And its pains are almost unbearable.

To erase your past is to dull your future
And to dull your future is to commit yourself to the sanguine fires of Hell.

Why Not?

The cracks in the wall
have meaning,
But you don't
understand them.

The keyhole
in the door
has a purpose,
But unless
you're a key
You don't know what it is.

A sticky piece of tape
will mess your mind,
Unless you take it off
your finger
and put
it on the wall.

II.
I walked
Down the street
to see a dead friend
who lives
near me,
But he was gone;
out to lunch,
I think.

Records turn on a
turntable
And have no meaning
except to be
listened to.

For the Life of Me

My dead friend
came back from lunch,
with a record he bought.
We put it on
his turntable
But couldn't listen to it,
Because his turntable is
Broke.

III.
I received
a phone call
from a deaf man
who wants to go home,
But his wife
won't let him because
he has short hair.

Franklin S White

I told him to buy
a wig
and not let her
know it,
He asked me if
I knew where he
could find a
blue and green
wig.

I said I
didn't know
So he hung
Up.

Next day he moved
in with my
Dead friend down
the street.

IV.
As a high-
school
graduate I
should
have ambition,
But I
Never went to
college.

Come Into My House, Death

Come into my house death
Close the door and walk about me
Because I fear you not
I do not fear you, because you cannot harm me.
Sure, you can strike down my friends,
And I will grieve,
But I can find new friends.

Come into my house death
And sit next to me
You cannot harm me, although try as you might.
If you wish you can kill the world and leave me by myself,
But this does not hurt me;
Because I still have myself.

Come into my house death
And cast your spells upon my walls
But still I will not fear you.
For as long as I am happy in myself you cannot harm me;
And I know that someday I must die;
But I do not fear death,
I welcome it.

Franklin S White

Sunglass Hobbits

Pill box hats and cough drop people
Drive themselves into community places of shame.
Crying spirits and half dead ghosts
Put 'Velvet Venus' on coke and rum
Because she did a good deed for the police chief;
Magic books upon freelance shelves are dusted by the upstairs chambermaid
While the downstairs butler quietly sneaks into the corner with the dean of women and plays solitaire.
Sunglass hobbits discover the truth about night,
But they tell no one.

The city mayor pencils in death on the bill to prevent birth control;
City council meets twice a week to play poker,
While the mayor stays at home sleeping with his daughter.
Everyone runs when the snow falls
But returns when the rain comes;
Stenographers record every-thing that happens while they watch each other take a bath.
Sunglass hobbits discover the truth about night
But they tell no one.

Saturday comes, but no one believes until Sunday passes;
Coils of spiritualism run wild among the leaves of summer
But passes underfoot of field mice,
Choking on tree bark and drinking dirty blood.
Reports on robberies come into the court house
And the prison warden doesn't except money from the community.
Sunglass hobbits discover the truth about night,
But they tell no one.

For the Life of Me

Invisible problems occur quite often
And surrender to the human eye;
Naked nymphs run around trying to see what clothes are made of
But they never wear them.
Because fabric of any type irritates their beautiful bodies.
Electronic, brains run the universe while plastic people look for togetherness;
They look among animals and other things of nature,
But never among other plastic people;
They don't know that togetherness breeds togetherness.
Sunglass hobbits discover the truth about night,
But they tell no one.

Post war feelings have changed,
But prewar hostilities grow worse each day;
Upon examining the facts of life, we find we must resort to the old world form in order to remain in sexual contact with our fellow humans,
Be they male or female; it makes no difference.
A power grant has been awarded to every man wants or needs one.
Sunglass hobbits discover the truth about night,
But they tell no one.

Extreme pain requires harsh treatment
But it can be achieved quite easily.
Being totally independent of one's own mind is very unnecessary,
If you are independent of all forces of nature you need not be independent from yourself;
Co-existence with people is good or bad,
It all depends on the individual.
Sunglass hobbits discover the truth about night,
But they tell no one.

Watch Out You're Crazy

Green, yellow,
orange, blue, or pink.
What color drives you-
drives you to the
doorstep of insanity.

Three cubes of ice;
in a tall glass of liquid.
They can and will
push you-
push you beyond
self-control.

A small room,
without doors or windows
can drive you-
drive you over
the doorstep of your senses.

I single flaw
In an otherwise
perfect surface
can take you-
take you far beyond
reality.

A bookshelf
lined with velvet,
with a single novel
of no purpose
will send you-
send you flying off
by yourself
to a world
which doesn't exist.

For the Life of Me

The books of the Bible
rend backwards
will help you-
help you on
your way to insanity.

So before they gang up
on you,
be careful and watch
yourself in every step.
Or you'll end up
in your own world-
your own little world
of insanity.

Argument: Two Sides

"And there's no more war"
Wouldn't it be bad.
No war, no peace-
No peace, no world.

"And there's no more war"
Wouldn't it be grand.
No war, no hate-
No hate, no killing-
No killing, no death without purpose.

"And there's no more war"
Is it good or bad?

Blind and Deaf

Blind as can be,
Without the sense of touch;
Deaf as possible,
And not able to feel.

Blind to murder and death,
Unable to feel out goodness;
Deaf to cries for help,
And not feeling for a helping hand.

Blind towards ignorance,
And not asking to be taught;
Deaf by choice,
Without the sense of touch.

Deaf and blind,
By choice not chance.

Color Me Red

Color me red
Blood red as in devil red
I'm blue
Because I'm sad in my sorrow

Color me red
As in rose red, I'm a sunflower
Try to, but won't
Because I don't want to
I'm tired, I'm sick
But doesn't matter no more
Because they're insane

Color me red
As in book read
I'm nearer to me than your skin
Don't care, don't wear
Clothes of same color
As my mind. Which can't be controlled
By outside force of gravity
Because I'm weightless and honorable.
My friends like me
An others hate me
I hate only one
And that's him, the one I hate

Color me red
As in dark pink red
Sunglasses are breakable
And so is my heart, it broke.
When I cry about in dark rooms
I shed no tears.
I have one minute of death,
Then I must live always;
So color me red.

For the Life of Me

The Mockingbird

The Mockingbird
Sings
mile playing Chopin on his back
He tries but can't talk
He's smart

The Mockingbird
Hears
All words of no meaning
The motherless child
And her son dine together
On air

The Mockingbird
Is all that he can
His beard drags the ground
He trips over his tail
And lands on his other foot
He's timely

The Mockingbird
Is knowing
But he tries
To be
But he can't

The Mockingbird
And his pet eagle
Play 'Robin Hood'
On the road to poverty
They're rich
With knowledge

Franklin S White

The Mockingbird
Pays attention to his pride
And lets nothing pass
His closed ear
While he sleeps unaware
Of his eagle

The Mockingbird
He tries and he does
But the eagle does not
They're partners
Alone and together
In what someone else does
Which doesn't concern them
At all

The Mockingbird
Died

For the Life of Me

Pre And Post

Life,
scans the horizon
looks for enjoyment,
but finds
emptiness.

Man,
lives until death
comes end takes,
then man goes
and dies.

Nature,
cries softly
and looks upon
her own beauty
then laughs loudly.

Deaths
absorbs all,
leaves none
and then fades,
until the next time.

Catch Me

Catch me if you want me,
Or I'll drift away like windblown snow,
But I'll return
In the event that your mind changes,
And you decide you want me.

Catch me if you need me-
Need me to give love that you want.
And I'll stay
Only as long as you want me,
Then once more I'll leave.

Catch me if you desire me,
Call me and I'll cone back,
Back to fulfill your desires
And when time comes when you desire me no more,
I'll fade into the past.

For the Life of Me

Come!

Come life, come death,
Come human sacrifice;
Come earth, come sun,
Come all solar space;
Enter the doorway and become new.

Come singers, come writers,
Come pencil and pen;
Come dancers, come actors,
Come all movies made;
Enter the doorway and become new.

Come dollars, come cents,
Come spenders of evil;
Come Gentile come Jew,
Come all man-kind;
Enter the doorway and become new.

Come dirt, come rock,
Come minerals of nature;
Come flowers, come trees,
Come all natures mysteries;
Enter the doorway and become new.

Come old, come young,
Come unborn;
Come man: come woman,
Come all to be born;
Enter the doorway and become new.

Franklin S White

Come windows, come doors,
Come houses and homes;
Come floors, come walls,
Come entire properties;
Enter the doorway and become new.

Come rapist, come murderer,
Come all crime;
Come law, come justice,
Come all courts;
Enter the doorway and become new.

Come wood, come steel,
Come man-made appliances;
Come rich, come poor,
Come,
Enter the doorway and become new.

Come lie, come truth,
Come words of mouth;
Come pestilence, come disease,
Come medical information;
Enter the doorway and become new.

Come nylon, come silk,
Come cloth;
Come skirt, come dress;
Come cleaners and pressers;
Enter the doorway and become new.

Come call girl, come pimp,
Come spenders of sin;
Come priest, come nun,
Come all religious believers;
Enter the doorway and become new.

For the Life of Me

Come books, come magazines,
Come readers of words;
Come teachers, come students,
Come all who need to learn;
Enter the doorway and become new.

Come records, come tape,
Come ears that listen;
Come pictures, come words,
Come all communications;
Enter the doorway and become new.

Come stamps, come letters,
Come readers of notes;
Come holes, come ditches,
Come all who labor;
Enter the doorway and become new.

Come one, come all,
Come, people, come!
Come you, come they,
Come all persons, places, and things;
Enter the doorway and become new.

Silent

It's twelve o'clock - noon;
I sit cross legged - asleep,
Aware only of dreams - silent.

Quickly I jump up - excited;
Slowly I sit down - exhausted,
Tired from being bored - silent.

Its Monday morning - tomorrow;
I awake from sleep - myself,
The time is Friday - silent.

Alone I die - together;
Beside myself I sit - unaware,
Without thinking I eat - silent.

Unnoticed by nature - living;
Understood in meaning - death,
Life and death - silent.

For the Life of Me

Like A...

Like A Buddhist Monk upon the windows
The rain does splatter.
And there are millions of untold stories behind deaths
But it doesn't matter.

Like a dying fly upon the malls
Is the way life must stand.
And even in Utopias dream of royalty,
Death must take a hand.

Like an unclosed door to a bottomless room,
Is the way that peace must be.
And even though the day must break,
No man really can be free.

Like a harnessed atom in a scientific worlds
A captured soldier must behave,
And while tomorrow's sun must set,
The world you cannot save.

Time

Time is and time does
What really is never was

Time is and time will be
Time for you and time for me

Time is here and time is there
But the time of day everyone must share

Time was written for a clock
But all you hear is a tick and a took

I can tell that time won't quit
I should know, I have plenty of it

For the Life of Me

To Exist Is To Die But Once

Ask me a question, any question you want;
No, don't ask me that one.
The rain outside comes from
Beneath the sky-high clouds.
It's a sunny day.

Don't talk to me,
Because I don't want to see your lies.
The brick and stone windows let in no sun;
But people don't care,
Because they are blind anyway;
Blind because they don't want to see.

"Twice is Like" is a song once written,
By a man who led two lives.
Thomas Hardy wrote a poem
That was never published,
So he wrote another.

Franklin S White

Here I

Here I stand,
And here I'll stay;
With mind in hand
My thoughts won't sway.

Here I'll be,
To have and hold;
Because from here I see
All men who are bold.

Here I am
But I will leave;
And the globe I'll span
With thought patterns to weave.

Here we are, and we'll always exist,
In a free country ruled by no iron fist.

Dance, Angels, Dance

Dance, angels, dance
Come fight with death;
You know you can't win.
Because death is ever present
And always existent,
But you try
So, dance, angels, dance

Sing, angels, sing
And try to put down war;
But you won't succeed.
War is always with us
And will never stop-
Never stop until man does.
So, sing, angels, sing.

Play, angels, play
Play your soft music
So that all man can hear;
But man cannot hear;
Because you speak truth
And man does not want truth,
He only wants other men's money.
So, play, angels, play.

Blood

Blood,
We hate to see you
We don't like you running freely
Especially running for no reason.
But man makes you run
And man stops you.

Blood,
Your color is so bright and beautiful
But we still hate you
You are not at fault completely
You are controlled by man
And man has authority over you.

Blood,
You are present everywhere
And you are happy to see war come
You are also happy to see accidents.
Man loves to see blood
Especially when it's not his.
Man cannot stomach to see his blood
Only someone else's.

A Mess of Words

The darkness of my room surrounds me,
As I sit looking at the central light.
There is a spider on my knee,
And I'm about to die from fright.

The books in the bookcase are being read,
But not by me, for I am asleep.
As I sleep, I dream of being dead,
And that's enough to make most people weep.

A university of thoughts are inside my brain,
And I'm trying to push them out.
So that I may sleep without strain,
And have a clear thought to follow dreams route.

If these past few lines mean nothing to you,
Then you're a fool for letting these words captivate you.

Franklin S White

The Room

Purple curtains on a bare green wall
With wood below, white paint above,
A broken clock on a table side stand
All alone in the corner my strings must stand.

They all make up the room.
Two red bulls on a chest of drawers
A horse head alone on a wall.
A closet and a hallway door
My clothes and shoes lay on the floor.
They all make up the room.

There's harmonica and guitar sheet music
And a doorstop for the door to rest.
There're two more horses over my head
And, oh yes, also a bed.
Together they all make up the room.

Untitled Symphony

The lone Ranger lives!
And the peace of man-kind is in danger;
"In danger of what?" you ask
How the hell should I know,
It's always in danger of something.

A bloodless vampire stalks the world
In search of human blood.
But he can't find any;
Everyone's gone plastic
And runs glue in their veins.
It's a harsh world for a vampire,

'Sex' has been outlawed in Cleveland,
They're trying to cut down on pigeons;
They want more people,
They need more taxes.

The 'gay boys' have been legalized,
All the women are hiding,
They want to see how the men make out without them.
The men don't care, they have the pigeons,
And they don't live in Cleveland.

Franklin S White

As The Night Is Silent

Sit down. Light passes through me
It shows my reflection on the walls.
Stand up. Darkness surrounds me
And blots my memory from all books.
As the night is silent

Plastic words from forgotten sentences.
Talk is meaningless. Mature people die
The dead rise at a given signal
Lie down. And to sleep you go.
As the night is silent.

Empty box.
It contains foolish records
All records can be broken.
Smoke filled rooms. They empty in time.
Old people are a burden to some.
As the night is silent:
So is the day beginning.

My Wonderings

Try as I might I cannot see by the eyes of my ears
By the light of day I walk the night
Wondering with my every step,
"When and where will I take my next,
And how long shall it Be?"

Watching the stars play tag under the moon
I see the sun shine
And wonder where it will hit next,
And pith what power shall it shine?

The doors and windows of my house shake
And the walls cry out for silence.
I sleep my day through
And wait for night to come,
But still I wonder.

But Never of the Future

As pipe smoke floats upwards towards the ceiling
I think of things past and present,
But never of the future.

I don't know what the future holds
And I really don't care,
I just sit and wait for it;
I know that it will come.

The winter season is standing outside my window.
Winter has come in the past
And is here now in the present,
It also will come in the future.

When I sleep tonight, I will dream-
Dream of the past and of the present
But never of the future.

Index

A Mess of Words 59
A Poem From The Heart 19
Ahaggarr (Straw Isle) 16
Argument: Two Sides 42
As The Night is Silent 62
Beauty 11
Blind and Deaf 43
Blood 58
But Never Of The Future 64
Catch Me 48
Color Me Red 44
Come Into My House, Death 37
Come! 49
Contemplation 7
Dance, Angeles, Dance 57
Death of One Man 21
Difference In People 13
Girls of Sin 24
Happening in One Day 1
Here I 56
I Light A Candle 25
I Loved You Once 6
If 18
Into Each Life 27
Life Goes On 29
Life, Death, and Love 32
Like A… 53
My Wonderings 62
Pre And Post 47
Silent 52
Snow And Wind 15
Sonnet To A Chair 26
Spanish Lace 3

Franklin S White

Substantial Circumstances 5
Sunglass Hobbits 38
The Death of Love 20
The End of the Earth 22
The Mockingbird 45
The Room 60
Time 54
To Exist Forever Is To Die But Once 55
Today and Tomorrow 23
Two Hearts (one Heart in Love) 2
Untitled Symphony 61
Watch Out: You're Crazy 40
We'll Meet 8
Wheels 30
When my Grave I Lay 9
Who Will Go With Me? 10
Why Not? 34
Withstand 14
Would it Make Any Difference? 12